The Little Book of BIG BLESSINGS

An Inspirational Journal

USA TODAY BESTSELLING AUTHOR
MISTY EVANS

The Little Book of Big Blessings ©2022 Misty Evans.
All Rights Reserved.
ISBN: 978-1-948686-54-9

Hello, Beautiful Soul!

Do you have five minutes (or less) every day to focus on the good stuff in your life?

I'm the mother of twins, and I run two businesses, along with being married to my soul mate of over thirty years and enjoying our three rescue pups. I love my life and find great joy in waking up every single day.

Life wasn't always good though, and I've struggled with various health and emotional issues since I was a child. I've kept journals since I was able to express myself, writing down my dreams, my plans and goals, and my disappointments. Journaling saved my life (many times). I used my journals as a catch-all for my stress and anxiety throughout life, and at times, it felt awesome to write down all the things that were going right for me, as well.

Still... When things were good, I often skipped journaling. "I'm too busy," I'd tell myself. "I'm too tired." You know what? Those things were true, but they were also self-fulfilling. What we tell ourselves has a sneaky way of manifesting in our life. The more I claimed I was too busy, it seemed the busier I became. After many years of self-healing for my inner child and learning about positive affirmations, I came to see that writing down the GOOD stuff was better for me.

Keeping a log of my accomplishments and daily wins, no matter how small, helped me feel confident. Writing down my dreams and wishes, no matter how silly or how out there they were, empowered me (especially when they often came true). Acknowledging all the things in my life that I was grateful for gave me a sense of peace and calm that I couldn't achieve when journaling about the not-so-great things that happened.

One of the benefits of journaling is the blessing hidden inside our words. When we write down a goal, our brain begins to set things in motion to accomplish it. When we write out a gratitude list, we shift negative energy into positive flow, freeing ourselves, even if it's a tiny bit, to create space for more joy.

Studies have shown that journaling can even strengthen your memory and give you a boost of self-confidence. Who doesn't need that?

Gratitude and journaling go hand in hand, and believe me, they create an unstoppable force to help you take back your power (instead of giving it away to external people, situations, and events). I've been trained in Shamanism, and empowerment is a core ideal.

Most people in our culture are disempowered, especially women and anyone seen as "other." Journaling and calling back your power heals your mind, body, and soul.

When we stay in a place of joy, we're in alignment with our purpose, and we find joy in being are true selves. On the page is where that can happen regularly, with no judgement or influence from outside factors.

It has been a long journey of self-discover for me, and using gratitude + journaling has helped me be emotionally strong and mentally focused. I've discovered I am more calm and centered when I keep my attention on all the wonderful blessings in my life and I choose to take a moment every day to honor the wins, in order to attract more. What we focus on increases, and I encourage you to focus on the good stuff!

Because of the people I've helped over the years, I've seen the transformations that can occur, and I 100% believe in the power of words. Whether we write them, say them mentally or out loud, they have POWER. Singing, humming, chanting – it all works to change our vibrational energy frequency. Raising that frequency, with any type of positive communication, is the key to connecting with love, finding true joy, and aligning with our amazing soul.

As an author of over seventy-five books, both fiction and non, I also know the power of words to entertain, to motivate, and to enlighten. The Little Book of Big Blessings is a combination of prayers, blessings, and inspirational journal prompts to walk the path home to your soul.

You can start with page one, or trust your intuition and flip to a random page. I've included blessings and prompts for different events, as well as everyday occurrences. The best way to cultivate journaling and gratitude into a positive habit is to keep it short and have fun. Break out your colored markers, pencils, etc., and make this journal YOURS.

Love and blessings,
Misty

Honor Life Every Day

Every day is a gift. Be grateful for your breath, for life. When you celebrate and honor each new day and the privilege of being present in the world, the Universe opens all kinds of doors for you.

Energize your day with the three morning blessings you'll find on the coming pages.

> Great Creator!
> Thank you for this day
> Thank you for my breath, for life itself.
> May my life be a celebration
> Thank you, thank you, thank you.

Take five minutes, and on the next page, write down what brings you joy and what you're grateful for.

Morning Affirmation

May love guide my thoughts today
May love guide my words today
May love guide my steps today

FINDING JOY

WHAT MAKES ME HAPPY?

WHAT AM I GRATEFUL FOR TODAY?

WHAT IS MY DEEPEST DESIRE TODAY?

Daily Help...

There are many guides in the unseen world ready and willing to help us each and every day. Whether you believe in angels, ascended masters, fairies, or simply something bigger and wiser than yourself, invoke the help of the guides and wisdom keepers in this and other dimensions.

Take a moment to imagine yourself at the head of a large conference table, the acting CEO of You, Inc.

Each day for the next week, write down what you need help with, then trust that the Universe will begin bringing you those people and resources who can make it happen!

Morning Affirmation

With every breath,
may I honor this day
May I be a channel
of love and healing
Thank you, thank
you, thank you.

FINDING JOY

WHAT MAKES ME HAPPY?

WHAT AM I GRATEFUL FOR TODAY?

WHAT IS MY DEEPEST DESIRE TODAY?

Let's talk about...

TODAY AM FEELING... ....
....
....
....

IF I COULD DO ANYTHING TODAY, I WOULD... ....
....
....
....

TODAY I AM LOOKING FORWARD TO... ....
....
....
....

MY AFFIRMATION TODAY ....
....
....
....

FINDING JOY

WHAT MAKES ME HAPPY?

WHAT AM I GRATEFUL FOR TODAY?

WHAT IS MY DEEPEST DESIRE TODAY?

What's on your to-do list, calendar, and schedule today?

What projects feel overwhelming?

What areas of your life could you use clarity in?

What issues are you having?

Morning Affirmation

May love guide my
thoughts today
May love guide my
words today
May love guide my
steps today

Daily Help...

Whether it's a project, relationship, or internal struggle, your guides and Higher Self are always available to you. They're like your own personal business team, your own relationships experts. There are those who are gifted with medical wisdom who can help with your health, others who can offer inspiration and motivation.

Here are a few of the situations that you can ask for help with:

Finding a new house, job, car, etc.
Technology glitches
Strained relationships
Seeking a new relationship
Project deadlines
Uncovering the right information at the right time
Learning a new skill
Recovering something that's lost

FINDING JOY

WHAT MAKES ME HAPPY?

WHAT AM I GRATEFUL FOR TODAY?

WHAT IS MY DEEPEST DESIRE TODAY?

Finding the Sacred in Each Day

Sacredness is an energy that's connected to Source, the Creator, and is present, like the creative energy of all things, in every moment of our day. We are spirits in a physical form, and both are sacred.

The sacred is in the ordinary—our breath, our health, our thoughts and interactions. Our relationship with ourselves, with others, and in nature all reflect the sacred essence of the Creator and conscious connectedness with our soul. We must make an effort to become aware of our own divinity in every given moment. To be mindful of the great wells of love, peace, and joy we can own and cultivate.

We yearn for more...more love, money, success, health. What we forget is we already inherently possess all we need. In spirit, there is no lack, and therefore no need to long for more. We fundamentally embody all that ever was and all that ever will be because we are holographs of the one Source of all things.

Nurturing our souls in small moments every day brings harmony and honors the sacred in every aspect of life. As we honor every thought, every step, every interaction, we feel more grounded and understand our life, and that of others with greater perspective and compassion.

All life is sacred. Begin finding your own inner spirit through meditation, music, creativity, or service. Connect your sacred self with nature and with a higher level of consciousness. Value yourself and see if you can find a few moments throughout the day to get still, tune into your soul, and offer a prayer or mantra.

Here is a short blessing to help you center and honor the sacred (based on the Reiki principles):

Just for today, I will trust my soul
Just for today, I will surrender to the Divine plan
Just for today, I will honor all living things, including myself
Just for today, I will speak my truth
Just for today, I will be grateful
And so it is

Here is a prayer to ask for help and guidance:

Angels, ancestors, and spirit guides
Use me as a channel for love and peace today
Show me the next step
Make your guidance clear
Thank you, thank you, thank you

What would you like divine intervention with today?

Honoring Home

The place where you live dictates much about your day-to-day life. The landscape, the weather, the foundation of your life. Connecting with the directions, the seasons, and what is often termed the Spirit of Place, helps you flow with the natural rhythms of the earth and cosmos, engaging these energies to support yours.

In shamanism, we form a strong allegiance with the elements and nature. We learn to fuse our essence with the air, wind, earth, and fire. We place great importance on celebrating and performing rituals to honor the planet, the spirit of Mother Nature, and of all creation. We are made from the elements of the earth and our physical bodies return to such when our soul departs. Being in tune with the cycles, respecting our bodies, which represent the physical land we live on, and creating a deep connection with the source of everything we have, is vital in living a healthy, prosperous life.

When was the last time you walked your property or put your bare feet on the ground? Do you know the types of wildlife, such as the birds, who inhabit your neighborhood? What kinds of trees?

Even if you live in an apartment or high-rise, you can still connect with the Spirit of Place by learning about the area and the history of the land where you reside. Take a walk around your neighborhood, watch the birds and the clouds. Learn about natural springs, rivers, and lakes. Breathe in the fresh air.

When moving to a new area, be sure to take a few moments to consider how the energy there feels, and where, in nature, it arises from.

On a regular basis, especially during the turning of the wheel of life, such as solstices and equinoxes, it's important to honor and bless where you live. The land, the house or dwelling, and the existential spirit and elementals who have been there long before you, and will continue long after you have passed through, will support you if you respect and honor them.

SPECIAL DAYS

For special days, such as solstice and equinox, call on the directions, seasons, and guides to honor you and your home:

Ancestors and spirits of the unseen elemental worlds,
I call upon the East and the season of spring
The rising sun and the element of air that remind me of new life
Bless this land and my home.
I call upon the South and the season of summer
The noonday sun and the element of fire that energize me
Bless this land and my home.
I call upon the West and the season of fall
The setting sun and the element of water that heals me
Bless this land and my home.
I call upon the North and the season of winter
The dark night sky and the element of earth that connects me to ancient wisdom
Bless this land and my home.
Thank you, thank you, thank you.

May this land be blessed
May the trees send down strong roots
And the flowers raise their faces to the sun
May the water flow pure and free
May the air blow clear and gentle
May my feet walk lightly, supported and nourished
By the grasses, the sand, the soil.
As I honor and call on the Spirit of Place to welcome me.
I honor and call on my own inner soul to embrace the seasons
The directions, and the Spirit that lives here.
May we walk together, work together, celebrate and support each other. Amen, a'ho, and so it is.

FINDING JOY

WHAT MAKES ME HAPPY?

WHAT AM I GRATEFUL FOR TODAY?

WHAT IS MY DEEPEST DESIRE TODAY?

INVOCATION TO THE SPIRIT GUIDES

Great Spirit, thank you for another day in this life
I honor the earth and all her abundance
I honor the call of my soul and its divine mission.

Guide me today. Set my footsteps right upon the path
Show my eyes what they need to see
Grace my heart with knowing.

May love guide my thoughts today
May love guide my words today
May love guide my steps today.

I am here to live a life of fullness and joy
Grant me the wisdom and clarity to be all I am meant to be
Show me the next right step and make it clear.

Thank you, thank you, thank you.
Amen, a'ho, and so it is.

HONORING GAIA

Mother, I feel you under my feet.
Mother, I feel your heartbeat.
Thank you for the abundance I have received.

Thank you for the life you and I have weaved.

With gratitude, I gather the fruits of seeds planted this spring.
With gratitude, I welcome the bounty you have yet to bring.

I am safe, I am held, I am supported.

Amen, a'ho, and so it is.

A NOTE FROM MISTY

I hope you've enjoyed this inspiration journal! Please reach out and let me know how I can support your journey.
Love & light,

Misty
crystalswithmisty@gmail.com

ABOUT MISTY

Energy healer, psychic, and shaman, Misty loves working with people on a soul level. Fascinated with past lives, she uses astrology, numerology, spirit guides, as well as good old common sense and her business acumen, to assist clients with resolving energy blocks and discovering their soul's purpose.

Before discovering her own life purpose, she went the traditional route and got a BA in Business, studied marketing and psychology, and thought about becoming a college professor. The Universe intervened and she ended up writing fiction. She is a USA TODAY bestselling author under both of her pen names, and runs her own publishing company.

Misty is a Crystal Reiki Master/Teacher, Usui Traditional Reiki Master, registered yoga teacher, Ayurvedic Specialist, and publishes under the names Misty Evans & Nyx Halliwell. She's married to her soul mate, has twin sons, and is totally enamored with her three rescue dogs.

Check out her books at www.readmistyevans.com and www.nyxhalliwell.com.

She sends out a newsletter once a month with all kinds of "woo woo" stuff in it, including energy tips and a crystal of the month. You can subscribe at www.crystalswithmisty.com